The Divine Pause

An invitation to reflect, recenter and reconnect
with your inner wisdom in a noisy world

Ally Rose

Editing and Design by Annick Ina Publishing

First edition, November 2019

ISBN: 9781701871526

www.thedivinepause.com

Table of Contents

This book is dedicated to:

My clients (past, present and future)—you continually teach me what it means to show up and courageously be seen. Thank you for allowing me to join you on your journeys.

My Cornerstone community—you are my people. Thank you for being a healing place where all are welcome—and that's not just something people say, it's actually walked out every day. Thank you for restoring my faith in church and what it means to belong to a community of believers.

My dearest friends and family—thank you for always believing in me and allowing me to borrow that belief during the times when I find it hard to believe in myself.

Sophia—you are my fiercest encourager. You see me in the messy middle and you love me, even there. Thank you for always being home and a safe place to land.

God—my Source and my Sustainer. Apart from you I am nothing and this book would never have been written. Thank you for the daily invitation to know your love more fully and understand what it means to dance through life with you.

A Note From The Author

AT THE END of 2017, I knew I had come to the end of myself. I could no longer live my life the way I had been living it. I got to a place where I knew without a doubt that something had to change.

Reaching this point meant being honest (uncomfortably honest) in some of my closest relationships, asking for help (like seeing my own counselor), pressing into and trusting in God like I never had before and remembering the sweetness of Divine Love.

I came to believe that if we have time to scroll on social media, we have time to pause and connect with Divine Love and our inner knowing. We live in a culture that glorifies busy. We've bought into the lie that busier is better. In doing so, we waste so much time on things that don't even matter to us.

I know that I'm not alone in my experience of feeling disconnected from myself. We live in a hyper-connected world, one where you can virtually connect with anyone, anywhere, anytime ... Yet we feel more disconnected than ever before. The hyper-connectedness and outward focus has led us to live lives where we're constantly looking to be filled from the outside rather than getting still and quiet, and connecting with that voice that's inside all of us that knows what we need.

The Divine Pause is about reconnecting to our Source, our inner knowing, to cultivate and create a life that is more authentic to who we truly are. It is about living life from the inside out as opposed to the outside in.

Since my realization in 2017, I've done a lot to take myself outside my comfort zone. My then-partner and I went through a conscious uncoupling, or as we now call it, our 'divine divorce,' where we have maintained a deep love and friendship with one another. I quit my safer, more secure agency job and started my own private practice, taking back power over my finances. And most importantly, I deepened my relationship with God/Source/Divine Love and have come home to myself.

I would not have been able to do any of these things without first acknowledging and accepting where I was. I had to be brutally honest with myself about the state of my health, my finances, my faith, my relationships, my work and why I wasn't fully living and loving my life.

So I looked inward.

This was not easy. Being truthful with ourselves and others is freaking hard work. It's easier to gloss over our discontent and blame others or blame circumstances for what we have failed to achieve.

But when you live like that, true change can never happen, because you're living under a false reality and your results will reflect that.

The Divine Pause is a gift of going within, from my heart to yours.

With love and gratitude,
Ally Rose

A Note On Terminology

IN THIS BOOK, I use many words to describe what I believe is the force of Love that is greater than all of us. My preferred term is God and I often use this word, but I recognize that the word 'God' turns a lot of people off because organized religion has caused a lot of pain in so many people's lives. Therefore, I also use the terms Inner Wisdom, Divine Love, Source and Higher Power interchangeably.

Further, I often refer to God as 'Him,' but I believe that God embodies both masculine and feminine qualities and that this Force of Love is bigger than labels and boxes. God is continually inviting us into the mystery of what it looks like to live our lives in a state of union.

Please use whatever term feels most comfortable and supportive for you. My prayer is that you would be willing to stay open as you read and notice how this Force of Love may be speaking to you through this book.

Introduction

THERE IS SO much noise, so many voices.

It's easy to lower your voice in the midst of the noise, to lose sight of your vision in the midst of all the striving.

Often, it becomes such a habit to fill those rare moments of silence with something that we don't even realize we're doing it.

And yet, God, your inner wisdom and your body are *always* speaking to you, giving you guidance.

The question is: are you listening?

As a mental health counselor and coach, when my clients come to me, they often feel stuck.

When we feel stuck in a particular area of our lives, it can feel overwhelming.

We don't know where to begin because it can feel like there are a million and one things we could do.

My encouragement is to always start with just one thing.

Just focus on one habit, pattern or behavior and leave the rest until later, after you've mastered that one thing.

This book was born from a place of feeling stuck in my own life. I had gotten to the end of myself. I was tired of portraying one life on the outside and feeling another way on the inside. I knew I could no longer live this way.

So I decided to be honest with myself and become my own best client.

I stopped doing *all* the things. I quit trying to please *all* the people. And I committed to doing *just one thing* . . . Cultivating a daily practice that could quiet the noise, all those voices outside of me, so that I could begin to see clearly again.

For me, this was a daily affirmation, a pause in my day to speak truth into my life, connect inwards and get back in touch with myself and Divine Love.

And it's no exaggeration to say it completely trans-formed my life.

Anyone who knows that they've gone astray from their authentic self, anyone who feels like they've been swept up in something outside of themselves that isn't truly them, anyone who wants to cut through the noise and make their way back home to Divine Love and to themselves, this is for you.

This book is an invitation to pause, reflect, recenter and reconnect with your inner wisdom in the midst of our noisy world.

How To Use This Book

THERE ARE MANY affirmations and space for reflection wrapped up in these pages. You could read this book from front to back, taking one affirmation a day to center yourself. You could open this book to a different page each day, trusting that you'll be guided to the right affirmation for you at any given time. You could meditate on one affirmation that resonates with you until you feel it's sunk into your bones.

It's up to you.

Really, there are no rules and you can't do it wrong.

I hope that you will highlight it, write in it, bookmark it, and share it with friends.

And however you decide to make your way through, I hope you find yourself and Love as you read.

Affirmations

I allow myself to transition gently into this new season of life.

My prayer is that you won't get caught up in the hustle and grind of this new season.

That you would know that it's okay to go at your own pace.

Inevitably, beautiful things will unfold when you honor that pace.

This doesn't mean that you stop planning or dreaming for what's to come . . .
In times of transition, sometimes what you need most is to anchor back into the flow that you've already created.

My reminder to you is that you can still . . .
Take the leap.
Quit the job.
Write the book.
Speak your truth.
Start the business.
Lose the weight.
Book the flight.
Say I love you.

Even if you don't hit the ground running.
Allow yourself to go slowly and with intentionality into this next phase.

It's okay to not have it all perfectly planned and figured out just yet.

Take your time to feel into and anchor in your own flow.
Try some new things, see how they feel and allow yourself to adjust accordingly as you go.

And remember that good things take time to grow.

I am learning to face my fears.

The thing about running from your fears is that everywhere you
go ... there they are.
You can't outrun them.
You only carry them with you.

What if you tried something different?
What if you stopped running?
What if you decided to stand still and come face-to-face with
one of your fears and bring it into the light?
When you shed light on what's been hiding in the dark, you take
away its power to control you.

Often, you'll realize there was nothing to be afraid of in the
first place.

You don't have to face them all.
And you don't have to do it all at once.
Just choose one.
And commit to slowly peeling back the layers until you get to the
core of what your fear is inviting you to uncover about yourself.

I choose to slow down enough to connect with the present moment.

Don't forfeit the joy found in small, sweet, simple moments on the journey because you're in a hurry to get to the destination.

My hope for you is that you are able to find moments to slow down.

To be truly present with yourself, the people you are with and in what you are doing.

And that by doing so, you get to experience real presence—the presence of Love.

I focus on my breathing to ground myself.

Today, take a moment to connect with your breath . . .
To pause.
To make space.
To collect your thoughts.
To remember.
To choose.
To face the next moment.

I choose to embrace uncertainty.

Often uncertainty feels just so uncomfortable, stressful and frustrating . . .

Because we want answers and we want them now.

What if instead of trying to push away the uncertainty and plow through it, we could embrace it?

Invite it in.
Sit with it.
Ask it what it's trying to teach you.
And listen.

Whenever I've been in long periods of waiting and uncertainty, I've heard God say . . .

I am here.
I am with you.
I am for you.

Give thanks in the waiting.
Trust that the pace of your life is perfect.
It's in the waiting that you're being refined and prepared for what's coming next.

So, if you're in a period of waiting or feeling the stress and anxiety rising up over the uncertainty, this message is for you too.
Where in your life do you need to embrace uncertainty?

In letting go, I find freedom.

What if instead of the fear of what we might lose, we valued what we might gain by letting go?

I embrace change and the hope of new beginnings.

Without change, we wouldn't get to experience new beginnings.

And yet, so often we fear and resist it.

Yes, there is grief and loss involved in change, in shedding skin, in letting go.
Allow yourself the time and space to grieve.
But don't stay stuck there.

When we hold on to what was, even if it's no longer working in our lives, we don't allow room for the life we deeply desire, the life we've been waiting for, to work its way into existence.

So here's to embracing change and new beginnings.
To letting go and trusting the process.
And to the beauty and magic that a fresh start brings.

Love, forgiveness and compassion are the foundation of my relationships.

We're human.
We fail, we fall, we make mistakes and we let each other down.
And then we get back up, try again and hopefully do better
next time.

When someone hurts us, or we have a disagreement or
miscommunication with someone, the easy way out is to withdraw,
wall off or go straight to anger, judgment, shame and blame.

You know what takes courage?

> Leaning in to love when you're afraid to fall.
> Staying when you want to run.
> Forgiving when you want to blame.
> Holding space for someone to share their heart.
> Expressing what you really want and need.

When we offer these things to the people we love, if they are
willing to join us there, we can enter more deeply into the dance
of intimacy.

May we have the courage to meet the people we care about
most in our lives with love, forgiveness and compassion.

IMPORTANT: I'm not talking about staying in an abusive
relationship or situation. If you are unsafe in any way (mentally,
physically, emotionally), the most courageous thing you can do is
leave and get the help and support you need.

It is safe to trust and follow my inner knowing.

Deep down, you know.
Deep down, we all know.

The trouble is we have given away our power.
We've tricked ourselves into believing that someone else outside of us knows what's best for us.

Give yourself the space to strip away all the layers of who you've been told you should be.
You are the expert on you.
Begin to cultivate that safety and trust within yourself.

And if you're having trouble figuring out how to begin to trust yourself, start small:

> Say "yes" when you really mean yes.
> Say "no" when you really mean no.

When you can trust yourself in the small decisions, it gets easier to trust yourself when it comes to the major ones.

Every day, I move closer to my true self.

Oh, hello . . . it's nice to meet you again.
You've been in hiding for far too long.

I am new today.

Note to self: It's okay if this season of your life got off to a weird start or hasn't gone exactly how you planned.
You are not your past.
You are not your struggle.
And you are allowed to start over whenever you need to.

I choose to practice the pause.

The old story desperately wants to keep playing out in your life . . . even if it's not serving you.

It wants to keep playing out because that's what it's always done, and it feels safe and comfortable.

But continuing to live out the old story isn't helping you become who you want to be.

It isn't leading you where you want to go.

When we choose to practice the pause, we interrupt the story.

We give ourselves the opportunity to see, choose and do something differently.

And if you want something different, you've got to *do* something different.

Old ways won't open new doors.

I surround myself with people who love and support me.

We're not supposed to do this life alone.
When you find your people,
Make sure you love them well.
Give thanks for your community.
And fight your battles together.

It is safe to explore.

To explore and discover all that God has for us, we must anchor into His love.

In order to anchor into that love, we must let go of any attachments that create a false sense of security in our lives and surrender them.

When we are firmly and deeply anchored into God's heart and His love, then we can explore without fear.

We can explore with wonder and freedom, like a small child who feels anchored in the safety and security of knowing she's loved.

As I walk through this week, I choose to see myself and others through the eyes of love.

Do you ever feel like we've reached a collective breaking point?

And we simply cannot bear . . .
More hate.
More violence.
More ugliness in the way we speak to one another.

Can you choose love knowing that, even with all of our differences, at our core, we all want and need to be loved?

My solitude is sacred.

Never apologize for needing time alone.

Sometimes, you have to spend time by yourself in order to come home to yourself.

Many are afraid of what they'll find if they spend time alone with themselves.

But what if by creating space to spend time alone, you find exactly what you've been looking for?

I am learning to surrender to love.

When you're in the middle of the messy, wild unknown . . .

Surrender.

When you wonder if you're going to be swallowed by the sea of your own emotions and sunk by the storms of your circumstances . . .

Surrender.

When all you can say is . . .
"I trust you.
I believe you and your promises to me.
Even though I don't see it.
Even though I don't understand . . ."

Surrender.

And God will meet you there and give you breath,
Over
And over
And over
Again,
So that you can make it through the next wave that comes crashing down.

If you're in the waiting or the middle of a storm, or your life is feeling kind of messy right now . . .

Surrender.

Love will carry you through.

I move boldly toward my dreams.

Change scares everyone, not just the person who's changing.

When you start to shift and make changes in your life, don't be surprised if friends and family don't understand you or are not as supportive as you thought they would be.

It's not because they don't want to be; it's because they've always known you as the you that you've always been.

And sometimes when you start to make positive changes in your life, it can make people feel uncomfortable and they may question why they don't have the courage to do the same themselves in their own lives. Or they fear they'll lose you.

Remember, someone else's negative reaction to your positive change is a lot more about their own wounding, fear and insecurity than it is about you.

No one else gets to live your life except you, and you playing small does not serve the world.

***I am committed to taking action
in spite of fear, trusting that I am
always divinely supported.***

There will always be another 'what if ...?' question ready and waiting to stop you in your tracks, to make you doubt moving forward, to give you an excuse for avoiding a risk.

Perhaps, before you're fully ready, it's time to start taking action toward the life you've always dreamed of living, knowing that if you wait until you're fully ready, you may never live it.

If it feels scary (and it will), start small.
But you've got to start.

Take one small step each day toward the life you desire, toward the dreams that have been planted in your heart.

And trust that ~~God~~ the multiverse will help you tweak and refine along the way.

I have everything I need to face any challenge or situation that comes my way.

I don't know all the details of what you've had to overcome to make it this far, but if you're reading this, it means you made it.

You survived.
You've done it before.
You'll do it again.

You are more courageous than you believe and more resilient than you give yourself credit for.

You got this!

I allow myself to rest.

Never underestimate the magical power of allowing yourself
to rest.

How many times have you found yourself saying . . .
"I'm going to push through and do just one more thing"?

Meanwhile, you've been running on empty for days or weeks
or months.
And that 'one more thing' you decided to take on only gets half-
done or gets done half-heartedly.

Sometimes the best thing we can do for ourselves and others is
to not do anything at all.

I am open to growth and transformation.

We say that we want to change, but new people, places, things and opportunities can't come into our lives through a closed mind or a closed heart.

Are you open?
Truly ask yourself this question.
"Am I open?"
And answer yourself honestly.

And if you're not, that's okay.

Ask yourself . . .

"What would I have to do or what would have to shift in my life in order to be more open to growth, change and transformation?" And see what comes up for you.

Oftentimes, we stay the same because we fear what others will think, or we fear losing relationships if we are no longer willing to do the things we've always done.

Asking questions and getting curious about yourself is one of the best ways that you can be kind and gentle in the process of personal growth and becoming more of who you want to be.

I stay in my own lane and focus on what's in front of me.

As you set intentions and goals for your life, take the time to consider if what you say you want to achieve is what you *actually* want, or if it's what you feel like you're *supposed* to want.

You will never win if you are trying to run someone else's race. Or if you are constantly looking at what everyone else is doing. You were not created to be someone else and run their race. You were created to be you, to run your own.

Stay in your own lane and run the race that's been set out for you.

I am holding space for myself.

In the middle of all of the outward momentum of living in this hectic world, all the giving and the going, make sure you take time to come home, go within and hold space for yourself.

ALLY ROSE

My presence is my connection to everything and everyone.

Reminder: It's really not about getting all the things.
Your presence with your people is the greatest gift of all.

I give myself permission.

When we're kids we have to ask for permission to do almost everything.

What I've learned is that we often carry into adulthood the idea of waiting for permission from someone outside of ourselves.

We're desperately waiting for someone to say, "I give you permission to <fill in the blank with a deep desire of your heart>."

The problem is that now it's up to you to give yourself permission . . .

To just be human, to make mistakes, to live a life that feels really amazing but can also look a little messy at the same time.

Where in your life do you need to write yourself a permission slip?

My life is right on schedule.

As you look back on your life, maybe you find yourself thinking things haven't gone exactly how you expected they would.

And that's okay.

Perhaps there were lessons that you needed to learn and layers that you needed to shed in preparation for what's to come.

You have to prepare the soil, before you can plant the seed, if you ever expect it to grow and fully bloom.

Know that there is no universal timeline that we all have
to follow.
Your timeline is divinely inspired.
You are exactly where you need to be, right now,
in this moment . . .
And nothing is off schedule.

God is co-authoring your story with you, and your story is good.

I embrace all parts of me.

We learn about our world through contrast.
We can't understand the light until we've experienced
the darkness.

There's a lot of pressure these days to stay super-high-vibe and
happy *all the time*.
But that's not the true human experience and it's okay to not
feel okay.

Sometimes we need to come face-to-face with our shadows,
and walk through them, to make our way into the light.

If you are struggling, please know that there is nothing wrong
with you and you are not alone.

Accept the invitation to meet Divine Love in the middle of what
feels like darkness.

Let Love lead you to the light.
You are something priceless.
You, and all of your light and darkness.

I trust my intuition to guide me in the right direction.

No matter what you've been told, you are the expert on yourself.
You know yourself better than anyone else.
There may be times when you need outside support
and guidance.
Someone who can help you see your situation more clearly.

But a good counselor or coach will never give you the answers,
tell you what to do or how to live your life . . .

Their job is to partner with you, hold space for you and help you
clear out all the noise, ideas and beliefs that aren't truly yours,
so that you can remember who you truly are, what you really
desire for your life and come home to yourself.

Trust your heart and intuition.
They want to be your guides.
Because deep down, you know.
Deep down, we all know.

It is safe to let go.

So, let go . . .

Of the life you thought you should have, but never truly wanted.

Of who you thought you should be, in order to be loved.

Of the lies that you believe, that give you a false sense of security, but are holding you back from living the life you truly desire.

It is safe to let go, because God is and will always be there.

I allow myself to take my time.

Don't rush.
Your path and pace are perfect for you.
It takes time to come back home to yourself.

I am honest with myself and others.

Step 1: Get honest with yourself.
Step 2: Get honest with others.

The secret is you can't skip step 1 because . . .

It's almost impossible to be honest with others if we are not honest with ourselves.

More often than not, the person we most need to face more than anyone else is ourselves.

There's something sacred about allowing yourself to find some internal rest and peace before you invite anyone else's voice and opinion into your process.

Honesty will set you free.

I choose to keep my thoughts focused on what I want to experience in my life.

What do you want to experience more of in your life?
When you look for something, you will find it.
And what you focus on grows.

It's kind of like when you get a new car and all of a sudden it feels like you see that car everywhere.

It's not because everyone else ran out and bought the same car at the same time.

It's because your new car is now what you are focusing on.

If you focus on all of the negativity and all that's going wrong in your world and the wider world, you will find more of that.

If you focus on finding joy, peace, kindness and love, you will find more of that.

Our minds are constantly looking to validate our thoughts.

This doesn't mean that negative thoughts won't pop into your mind, but you can notice them without holding onto them. Then flip the switch.

You don't have to believe everything your mind tells you.

Try it out as an experiment this week.
Start to take back your power, tame your thoughts and choose where to place your focus.

I am brave.

Be brave, dear one.
Keep going.
It's worth it.
You're worth it.

I am learning to speak my truth.

People are not mind-readers. We need to tell them what we want and need.

I know that this can be a difficult thing to do.
Because when we speak our truth, there's always the chance that those around us might not be ready or able to meet us there.

But when you express what you want and need, you communicate to yourself that you matter . . .
Regardless of whether or not someone else is ready to hear you or hold space for you.

If it feels scary to speak your truth, start small.
Say yes when you truly want something, but know you can say no when you truly mean no.

You are worthy of being seen, heard and known.

I allow myself to start again whenever I need to.

How often do we say, I'll start eating better on Monday? Or announce in January that we're giving something up as a resolution?

I love the fresh start of a new week, a new month or new year, but my mindset around 'starting over' has shifted.

Whereas I used to find myself waiting until an arbitrary date on the calendar to get started on my dreams and desires, now I look at it like this:

Every single day you have a chance to choose a new and different way of moving, being and showing up in your world.

You can start again whenever you need to.

I find joy in the journey.

I'm convinced that life is more about the journey, the process of discovering, becoming and owning who we've been created to be, than it is about reaching any destination.

We can complain and get upset because we're not 'there' yet . . .

Or we can recognize that there is no 'there' and choose to find joy in the journey instead.

I am strong.

What if all the things you once thought made you weak have actually made you stronger?

I am thankful for it all.

The highs.
The lows.
The blessings.
The lessons.
The setbacks.
The comebacks.
The love.
The pain.
The everything.
Be thankful for it all, because it's about learning and growing from everything that comes our way.

I wait patiently, because life unfolds at the perfect speed.

Be patient.
When we rush,
When we're in a hurry,
When we try and force things to happen,
It's easy to settle for less than the best.
Less than we truly desire,
Less than we truly deserve . . .
But good things often take time to grow.
And miracles . . .
They're worth waiting for.

I allow myself to shine.

You were born to shine your light bright.
You never know how many people may find their way home and
out of the darkness because you chose not to give up.

I choose to see the good in people.

My hope is that we can try to remember that underneath all of the layers and the labels that we put on people—Republican, Democrat, black, white, Christian, Muslim, Jewish, gay, straight— there is goodness there.

It's what is always there at our core.
It's the truth of who we really are.
May we choose to see the good in the people we meet . . .
Not just during emergencies or times of distress.
Not just during the holidays,
But every single day.

I am enough just as I am.

Whatever you did,
You are enough.

Whatever you didn't get done,
You are enough.

Whatever you will do,
You are enough.

I release the fear of failure.

Do you fear failure?
Are you a prisoner to this fear?

If so, it will stop you from ever stepping out and making bold
moves that get you closer to your desired life.

The thing is we can never be 100% certain of how anything will
turn out.
And if we never take risks or step out in faith
Without having to see how it will all come together,
We end up missing out on actually living life.

Can you look at failure as a learning opportunity?
What if the only way that you could ever truly fail is by not
getting back up when you fall?

What would you do differently in your life if you could shift your
perspective and release this fear?

I am exactly where I am supposed to be.

Life is our classroom and each one of us has our own
soul curriculum.

There are lessons we need to learn by being exactly where we
are right now, in *this* moment and in *this* situation, in order to
become the people we're meant to be and create the lives
we're meant to live.

Have faith in the process.
Embrace the unfolding of it all.
Enjoy the beauty of becoming who you were always meant
to be.

I release my need to constantly have the approval of others.

Are you living your life based on what you truly desire?
Or are you living your life based on what your friends, your family or some random stranger on social media might say or think about you?

No matter what you do, you will never make everyone happy . . .

Even when you're doing your best, someone will most likely still find fault with something you're doing, ultimately leaving you upset or unhappy.

Release yourself from the prison of people-pleasing.

My power and peace are always in the present moment.

To bring myself back to the present moment when my mind is drifting, I'll gently say to myself:

"There is nothing more important than this moment . . ."
Or
"There is nothing more important than the person in front of me right now . . ."

It is centering and magical.
And a reminder that all we ever really have is this moment, right now.

I am committed to doing the work I need to do in order to heal.

Here's the thing, my friend . . .
The work works . . . if you actually do the work.

The secret is you actually have to do the work and no one else can do it for you.

No one can heal you.
No one can save you.
No one can make you whole.
That's up to you.

Nothing brings me more joy than when someone comes into a counseling session and says, often in shock, "This stuff actually works!"
Often they thank me, as their counselor.

And yes, holding a safe space and offering tools to use is part of the process . . .
But *they* chose to commit to their growth.
They chose to commit to their healing.
They chose to do the work beyond our session.
Nobody could do it for them.

Is it time to recommit . . .

. . . To yourself?
. . . To your own growth?
. . . To your own healing?

ALLY ROSE

. . . To doing your own work?

I did this:
I've pulled the parts of myself that I've hated, hidden and denied
close to me like little children, staring them straight in the eyes
and telling them that I love them, even though they've been
painful and hard to look at.

I did this because I don't just want to talk the talk.
I want to walk the walk.

And I never want to ask someone to do anything that I wouldn't
do myself.
And let me tell you something . . .
The work works, y'all.

So show up for yourself.
Do the work.
Do it scared.
Do it when you don't believe in yourself.
Do it even when you're not sure if it will work.
Because eventually it does.
And you're worth it.

Every new day, I am a new me.

Let go of yesterday and any regrets, perceived failures
or mistakes.
Learn from them, but don't live there.

You don't live in the past.
You live in the present.

And your present self can always change your future
One moment,
One step,
One decision at a time.

Today is a fresh new beginning and you get to *choose* who you
will be!

What's one goal or intention that you want to achieve before the
end of the week?

I am filled with hope for all that is to come.

In the midst of the challenges of life, it can be hard to continue to have hope.

When you feel like you've reached a breaking point, remember that when something breaks or cracks, that's when the light pours in.

The more our hearts continue to break open about what's going on in the world around us, the more the light that's pouring in will ignite a spark within us and fuel the fire for change.

We can begin to change our lives and our communities in our own small ways:

> Volunteer with or donate to an organization that's doing good in your community.
> Simply say hello and smile at a neighbor as you pass them on the street.
> Make a phone call to someone you haven't seen in a while to check in on them.
> Compliment someone.
> Hug your friends and family a little longer.
> Take a meal to someone who needs it.

We can't wait for someone out there to change our lives.
No one can do everything, but we can all do one small thing.

I am moving forward.

Because we live so much of life in the small, quiet, seemingly insignificant moments that don't feel huge or life-altering, sometimes we're moving forward even when it feels like we're standing still.

But those small moments, those small decisions, those little lessons you are learning along the way are the pieces that make up the picture of who you are becoming.

So just keep going.
Keep moving forward,
Walking your journey, step by step,
Building your life, moment by moment.

And when you're feeling frustrated in the waiting, remember that ~~God~~ *the Universe* loves us in the details of our lives and that everything is unfolding at the perfect speed, in the perfect timing.

I choose to find deep peace within myself.

Finding peace is an inside out job.
We need to stop searching outside ourselves and looking to others for our peace, because we won't ever find it there.

Peace is a choice that we get to make, just like choosing to get caught up in fear or worry.

The act of choosing gives us back our power, rather than giving it away to circumstances, other people or fleeting and often irrational emotions.

When faced with challenges or difficulty, we may feel disconnected from a peaceful inner space, but the power is in recognizing that the peace is always there and available to you.

I forgive myself.

Forgiveness is not always easy.

But if you want to move forward in life, allow yourself the space to 'feel the feels' around the situation . . .

Then learn from it and let it go.
There's nothing you can do about it now.
Commit to moving forward in a different way.

Forgive yourself as many times as you need in order to make peace with yourself and set yourself free.

I am most powerful when I'm my true self.

Have you ever tried fitting into other people's boxes?
Have you ever tried to be someone else because you thought that was the only way you'd be loved or accepted?

This can be uncomfortable and exhausting.

I know firsthand because I tried to be someone I wasn't for years . . .

When you're playing a part, the real you is often rebelling, trying to escape and make its way to the surface.

Stepping into your own power and being more authentically yourself is terrifying, yet it's also one of the most freeing and life-giving experiences you could ever have.

So, be you.
Because being you is your superpower.

I receive with gratitude all that this new day has to offer me.

Today, choose to step into the flow . . .
Say *yes* with gratitude to receiving all the good things that life has to offer you.

When you open yourself up to receiving and allow your cup to be filled, you can then pour out from your overflow and trust that your cup will be refilled again.

ALLY ROSE

***I am patient and kind with myself and others
as we discover the truth of who we really are.***

We cannot rush the process, our own or anyone else's.

Sometimes when you've done everything that you can do at this moment, the only thing left to do is trust and wait.

And choose wonder in the waiting.

70

I am learning to love myself.

Self-love and learning how to love yourself is the foundation of the work that I do as a counselor and coach.

I've seen people fully commit and immerse themselves in the process of learning how to love themselves and it totally changes every area of their lives.

A lot of the resistance I see around self-love comes down to one question:

Isn't self-love selfish or egotistical?

Far from it . . .

First, self-love does not mean valuing others less. It means recognizing that you have equal importance, because so often the love that we pour out for others, we never give to ourselves.

We are not better or worse than anyone else. And we deserve all the love that we are willing to give to others.

And second, self-love is a way of being united in agreement with your Creator. It's a way of saying, "Yes, I see what you've created and I believe you've created something good."

It's a process and a journey to love yourself. It doesn't happen overnight, so take it step-by-step and be gentle with yourself in the process. What's one thing you can start doing to love yourself well?

I ask for and am open to receiving the help I need.

It's okay to not be okay.
It's also okay to ask for help.
You are fully loved even when you're not okay.

Having someone help you doesn't mean you've failed.
We were created for community and connection.
We are not supposed to do this life alone.

If you need someone, please reach out.
And even if they're not in crisis, could you take some time this week to ask a friend or family member, "How are you?"

And if they say, "I'm fine," maybe press a little and ask, "How are you, really?"

Then if they decide to share their deep thoughts, really listen.

Many of us live behind the mask of "I'm fine and everything is okay" even when we're not fine or nothing is okay.

That question, asked by a dear friend on a regular basis, has the power to change a life.
It gives people the permission and space to be more fully seen, heard, known and ultimately loved.

I am surrounded by love.

Can't find or feel it?
Love is not always big, bold and flashy.
Look for it in the ordinary, everyday, small things.
God loves us in the details of our lives.

I give myself permission to shine.

Goal: Be more like the sun.

Sometimes we dim our light because we're afraid we'll be too much.
But for the person who is in complete darkness, your love and light is exactly what they need.

Shine bright, my friend.
We need your light, now more than ever.

When you've been in the middle of a dark time, who has been the light in your life?
In what small way can you let your love, light, truth and compassion shine in someone else's life?

I am thankful for simply being alive.

The world may not always be an easy place to live, but there is always something to be grateful for.

What I've found in the middle of a busy, stressful or difficult season is that it's often in the small, sweet, simple moments where life reminds me how beautiful it really is.

What was the highlight of your day?

What are you most grateful for this week?
Where have you recently been reminded about the beauty of life?

I celebrate my strength.

To those of you who show up every day for yourself and the people you love, even when you're fighting silent battles behind the scenes and it feels dark and difficult . . .
I celebrate your strength.

For all the times I chose not to give up, when I decided instead to trust, have faith and remain . . .
I celebrate my strength.

To my clients who are committed to their growth and healing . . .

I celebrate your strength.

Give yourself some credit for the progress you have made and all you've overcome.

Where can you acknowledge and celebrate your strength today?

I love myself and allow myself to be fully loved.

Life has a way of teaching you the incredibly transforming and healing power of love when you are open to allowing it in.

When you are willing to receive it and give it freely and without fear.

Maybe you've always known on a head level that love is powerful, but to get it on a heart level, that is something else entirely.

Something shifts and changes in our lives when we allow ourselves to fully embrace and experience something. When it becomes a part of our being.

Let yourself be fully loved.
It has the power to change your life.

I accept the truth even when it is difficult.

Growth and change begin with acceptance.
Accepting the truth of a situation doesn't mean being in
agreement with it.
Accepting the truth of a situation doesn't make it any
less painful.
But accepting the truth will set you free.

It is only when we get really honest with ourselves about what is
and where we are—in our health and fitness, our finances, our
career or business and our relationships—that we can make a
plan to move forward in new and better ways.

Otherwise, we tend to end up repeating the same painful
patterns and cycles over and over again . . . wondering why
nothing is changing.

Where in your life do you need to accept the truth so that you
can make a plan to move forward in a new, different and
better way?

I recommit to my goals, my vision, my why and myself, because I'm worth it.

God loves it when we say yes to Him, whether it's for the first time or the 400th time, whether we said yes to Him years ago or just yesterday.

What are you being called to say yes to again or for the very first time?

Has your vision for your life shifted and changed from the beginning of the year?

Have you lost your excitement and passion around a goal that is actually really important to you?

Are you being called to recommit to something for the 274th time today?

Or are you being called to commit to something new for the very first time?

Slow down enough to not miss the moment of what you're being called to.

Recommit.
Say yes again.
And again.
And again.
As many times as you need to . . .
Because you're worth it.

I commit to giving myself what I need.

What do you need more of?

So many of us are on healing journeys.
It's important to take really good care of ourselves, especially as we heal.

I encourage you to slow down, check in, get quiet and listen for what you really need.
You might be surprised at what comes up!

Then try to commit to giving that to yourself as best as you can.

To you and everyone on a healing journey right now,
I see you.
I hear you.
I'm with you.

I believe in myself.

Sometimes all it takes is one moment of courageously believing in ourselves to completely change the direction of our lives.

Take the leap. ✓
Quit the job. ✓
Write the book. ✓
Speak your truth. ✓
Start the business.
Book the flight. ✓
Say I love you. ✓
You got this!

I embrace all parts of me and release the need to be perfect.

Kintsugi—"the art of precious scars"—is the Japanese art of fixing broken pottery with a special lacquer dusted with powdered gold, silver or platinum.

Beautiful seams of gold glint in the cracks of ceramicware, giving a unique appearance to the piece.

This repair method *celebrates* each artifact's unique history by emphasizing its fractures and breaks instead of hiding or disguising them.

Kintsugi often makes the repaired piece even more beautiful than the original, revitalizing it with new life.

A reminder for anyone who is feeling broken or whose life feels beyond repair:

The broken pieces of your life can be put back together and built into something more beautiful than you ever thought possible.

I choose to believe that amazing opportunities exist for me in every area of my life, and am open to seeing them.

There's always an infinite flow of opportunities around us.

To love and be loved.
To give and receive.
To serve and lead.

Each day, we're being invited to step into the river of opportunities and flow with it.
May we have increased awareness around the ways that Divine Love is already showing up in our lives, inviting us to join in the dance and the courage to say yes to the invitation.

I allow myself to take risks.

Great love.
Great adventure.
Great achievement.
Great transformation.
These often involve great risk.
Let go.
Let yourself fully live.

I am patient with myself as I grow and change.

In a culture that's obsessed with quick fixes and instant gratification, it can be hard to remember that good things rarely happen overnight.

Change requires that we make a decision, then take the leap.

And yes, making this decision can happen in an instant or at some kind of turning-point moment,
But it takes time to cultivate and nurture the transformation taking place on the inside.

Day by day.
Moment by moment.
One foot in front of the other.

Each day, we get to decide again to water the seeds of change that have been planted within us.
May we have patience with ourselves in the process of becoming more fully who we've been created to be.

I allow myself to grow and change.

When you're thinking about or in the process of making big changes in your life,
It can feel both terrifying and exciting all at once.

And there's definitely value in seeking wisdom and guidance from trusted mentors and friends.
But at a certain point, you just have to trust yourself.
You have to realize that no one else can do it for you.
You have to give yourself permission ...

> To release the guilt around wanting more from your life and your relationships.
> To make a decision and take the leap.
> To not be perfect or have to get it right all the time.
> To stumble, fall down, realize that you didn't die and get back up and try again.

You don't always have to know the how.
You just have to know that you can.

I choose to remain calm and centered, even when there is chaos around me.

Divine Love is our anchor in this often-chaotic sea of life.

When we remember that we are fully loved, fully worthy and that nothing can separate us from that anchor of love, we can handle whatever comes our way.

As you walk through your life, may you remember who you are and whose you are.

And live and love from that place.

I give myself the time and space I need to heal.

Things I've learned about healing:

1. You've got to feel it to heal it.

    Often, we may try to move through healing on a head level, attempting to bypass healing on a heart level.

    Or we stuff our feelings so far down and out of sight, hoping that they'll just magically disappear . . .

    I hate to break it to you, but they don't. No matter how far down you stuff them, they'll find a way to resurface.

2. It doesn't matter what anyone else says about you. It only matters what God and *you* say about you.

3. It is not about trying to get someone else to choose you. You have already been chosen by Divine Love. And you've got to learn how to choose yourself too.

4. Your calling and your purpose are bigger than the pain. Remember that you will get through this; it won't last forever.

Sit with your pain and sadness.
Look at it.
Lean into it.
Learn from it and let it make you stronger.
But don't let it keep you stuck.

THE DIVINE PAUSE

If you're 'in it' right now, please know that you're not alone.
Give yourself time and space to heal, because you're worth it!
Sending you so much love for the journey.

I am learning to speak my truth.

Stepping into vulnerability can be one of the most terrifying and painful things you ever experienced . . .

Yet it can also be one of the most freeing experiences, bringing you closer to the people you love and to the heart of God.

The more you share your truth, the easier it will become and the more freedom you will experience.

Because every time we speak our truth, a piece of our shame story—the 'I am bad' or 'I am not enough' story—dies.

Acknowledging and accepting parts of ourselves that we've kept hidden gives us life and breath.

You do not have to make some grandiose announcement to all your friends and family or on social media in order to speak your truth, because not everyone will be able to hold it or handle it. Start small and share with just one person you know you can trust.

Where have you been holding back?
Where do you need to speak more of your truth?

I trust in my ability to create a life I love.

It's not all on me.

It's not all on you.

Ultimately, God's got us.

But a huge piece of this is in *trusting* yourself to care for you in a way that *only* you can do.

This can mean creating habits in your life that are life-affirming and not soul-depleting.

What's one thing you're committed to doing today, this week or this month to take really good care of yourself; something that will move you closer to living a life you love?

I let go of worrying about things outside my control.

Sometimes we end up carrying or holding on to things that were never ours to pick up in the first place.

One of my favorite ways to end the week is to check in with myself and ask:

"What am I carrying that's not mine? What's weighing me down? What is outside of my control?"
And then I try to let it go . . .

I get it.
Letting go is easier said than done.
But here are some ways that you can practice letting go:

> Praying and giving it up to God or your higher power.
> Writing it down and then ripping it up.
> Visualizing putting it in a balloon and releasing it.
> Imagining giving it back to the person it belongs to.

What do you need to let go of?

I choose to rest and trust in divine timing.

Rest.
Trust.
Be.
Allow.

These things are hard to do in our always striving, pushing, forcing, manipulating, controlling, 'make it happen' culture.

I've learned the hard way what happens when I get impatient and try to force things to happen according to my own plans.

God's timing is always so much better and sweeter than our own.

So, rest and trust in the waiting . . .
And know it will be worth it.

I always have the power to choose.

Have you ever made a choice to make a huge shift in your life, then when you settled into that choice, realized you were miserable?

Perhaps deep down, you made the choice from a place of feeling like you needed to prove something to others.

This is typically a red flag that you're probably not making a choice you'll be happy with.

In the past, I would tell myself that I'd made a choice and now I had to live with it, meaning that I needed to suffer with my choice for this extended period of time.

It would almost feel like I needed to punish myself for not making the right choice in the first place or that I needed to prove how strong I was by enduring.

Sometimes the choices we make *are* irreversible.
Sometimes we do have to suffer some consequences.
But lots of choices are not irreversible.

We don't have to punish ourselves or stay stuck in something just to prove something to ourselves or anyone else.

And sometimes we have to choose the wrong thing just to know it wasn't right for us.

We tend to forget that our greatest power is our power to choose.

THE DIVINE PAUSE

And every day that we wake up, we get to choose again.
To remain the same or do something different.

So choose to release yourself from:
> Feeling powerless.
> Feeling like you must endure in order to prove a point.
> Guilt, shame and self-judgment.

And as soon you do, you'll feel the weight lift from your chest
and you'll know that you are making the best choice for you.

Where in your life do you need to remind yourself that you always
have the power to choose again, to choose something different
or new?

I choose to live a life filled with love.

Death has a way of causing you to pause and think about your own story.

Why will people remember you?
What stories will they tell about you?

How will they remember the way you made them feel?
Will your people know you loved them deeply?

Death makes you realize:

If you don't like the story you've been writing, if you woke up this morning, there's still time to change the ending . . .

If you're lucky enough to have people in your life that you love deeply, you don't have to let fear hold you back from letting them know.

I embrace change and the hope of new beginnings.

So often we fear and resist change, but without change, we wouldn't get to experience new beginnings.

I believe our lives mirror the seasons.

In the fall, as the leaves change color, fall to the ground and let go of all they've held onto in the previous season, they are a reminder that change doesn't have to be painful.

It can be a beautiful part of life.

The trees don't try and hold onto their leaves.
They don't resist that winter is coming.
They trust in the process and rest in knowing that they'll be made new again next season.

So here's to embracing change and new beginnings, to letting go and trusting the process and to the beauty and magic that a fresh start brings.

I choose to live in the present moment because that is all that truly exists.

Life is a mosaic of moments.

In a moment, we can experience deep love.
In a moment, we can experience great loss.
In a moment, we can make a choice or receive news that changes our lives forever.

You don't want to miss the moment because you were too busy worrying about the past or the future.

Let's make the moments of our lives mindful and meaningful.

Love is flowing to me and through me in abundance.

There is no shortage of love.
Believe that you can give and receive love freely, because there is more than enough to go around.

I focus on my breathing to ground myself.

Today, take a moment to connect with your breath . . .
To pause.
To make space.
To collect your thoughts.
To remember.
To choose.
To face the next moment.

***I am worthy of and open to receiving
all the love, support and abundance
that life has to offer me.***

The truth is love and good things will still come your way even if
you don't believe you deserve them.
But if you don't believe you deserve them, you may end up
subconsciously rejecting good things, thus never actually
allowing yourself to experience them.
In order to embrace and fully experience the goodness that's
always on its way to you, you have to believe that you
are worthy.
And you are.

I choose to have faith in the way things are unfolding, instead of fearing the unknown.

When big changes and new opportunities are on the horizon, with lots of question marks around how it will all work out, it's easy to fall into fearful thinking.

Do we really believe what we say we believe?
Or are we just speaking it with our mouths?

Sometimes we say we have faith and feel fully supported, but we are not actually walking it out.
We let fear hold us back.

F-E-A-R
It has two meanings.

Forget Everything And Run
OR
Face Everything And Rise

None of us can escape fear, but we get to choose which one we will accept as our reality. What will you choose?

I choose to embrace uncertainty.

Often uncertainty just feels so uncomfortable, stressful
and frustrating.
Because we want answers and we want them now.
What if instead of trying to push away the uncertainty, and plow
through it, we could embrace it?

When I have experienced uncertainty, I have heard ~~God~~ say: *my inner Knowing to*

> Give thanks in the waiting.
> Trust that the pace of your life is perfect.
> It's in the waiting that you're being refined and prepared for
what's coming next.

So, if you're in a period of waiting or feeling stress and anxiety
rising up around any uncertainty in your life right now, this
message is for you too.
Where in your life do you need to embrace uncertainty?

I commit to giving myself what I need.

What do you need to give yourself today, this week, this month?

Is it time?

Space?
A break?
Kindness?
Patience?
A couple more moments of silence than you'd normally allow yourself to have?
Do you need to ask for help in some area of your life?

Get still, listen in and hear what your intuition says you really need.
You might be surprised by what you hear.
Then, when the time is right, commit to gifting yourself something that helps you meet that need for yourself.

I make time for rest and play.

Rest and play are not just for kids.
Rest and play are necessary for all of us who desire to live more joyful and meaningful lives.

When I rest, I'm refilled—first for me and then for others, so that I can serve them from a place of fulfillment.

When I play, I connect to childlike curiosity and wonder.
Curiosity and play keeps us alive, interested and interesting.

But these things don't happen by accident.
There will always be more to-dos to check off our lists, something that seems more important than napping, getting away from it all, or doing something just because it's fun.

This means we have to be intentional about cultivating rest and play in our lives.
We need to let go of wearing busyness, exhaustion and productivity as badges of honor and become more intentional.

This may feel uncomfortable at first.
You might even feel guilty for taking this time for you, because you'll be going against the grain of all that you may have been taught about your worth and value.

As always, start small and build from there.
Where can you carve out just one hour of time where you can play and explore, or spend time just being and not doing?

I choose to see myself and those around me through the eyes of Love.

When we're feeling a bit off, we can often be more critical of ourselves and others.

It's important to remember:

> Your day is not decided by one single moment.
> Life is a series of choices that *you* get to make.
> You don't have to be held hostage by your feelings.
> In every moment, you can choose again, and that you can choose something new and different.

So choose love, because the 'Love lens' changes everything.

I believe in miracles.

How can you begin to shift your perspective around your situation and your story in order to experience more miracles?

This could mean, when things 'go wrong' in life, rather than feeling like you're being punished, could you look at challenges and adversity as blessings in disguise?

Or you could look at past choices that you and others have made with more love and compassion?

Compassion for past mistakes has been a game-changer in my life.
It has allowed me to experience more peace and love in some of my closest relationships than I'd experienced in a long time,
And this truly feels like a miracle.
Where do you need to experience a miracle in your life?
How can you shift your perspective from fear to love?

I express myself truthfully and clearly.

We teach people how to treat us by what we allow.
When you express what you want and need, you communicate to
yourself that you matter.
What I've learned is that the *right* people, the people who are
your people, want to know the real you.
Not some fake, cookie-cutter version of who you've molded
yourself into in order to please them.
If it feels too much to start speaking your truth, take baby steps.
Say yes only when you really mean yes.
Say no when you don't.
It's okay to want to be seen and heard.
You are worthy of being known.

I enter into this new season filled with gratitude.

Gratitude changes everything.
In an instant, it shifts your energy toward abundance, goodness and more than enough . . .
As you enter into a new season, what are you grateful for?

I trust myself to make the best decisions for me.

Do you trust yourself?

It's a question I often ask my counseling and coaching clients. And a question I ask myself too.

The truth is most people don't.
When we don't trust ourselves, we give away our power.

Often, this manifests as constantly looking for other people to validate our choices or make decisions for us.

It can feel a little like being a boat getting tossed about in the waves.
Never fully secure or balanced.
Never fully able to get solid footing.

When you start to build trust with yourself, by doing little things like following through with the commitments you've made or setting boundaries and sticking to them, you root your anchor a little more firmly into the ground.

That way, when the waves come, when life happens, your boat might be rocked a bit . . .

But it won't capsize.
You won't get thrown overboard.
You won't drown in uncertainty.
You'll be rooted in self-trust, knowing you can safely make it through the storm.

My life and story are divinely guided and inspired.

Are you struggling with surrendering your attachment to the timelines you've decided you must follow?

Are you feeling the pressure to be, do or have something by a certain point in your life?

Does it feel difficult to trust that the story being written in you and through you is good, even if it doesn't look how you thought it would or should?

If so, you're not alone.

It's easy to believe that if we're not where we thought we would be by now:

> There's something wrong with us.
> We've been forgotten.
> Those parts of our stories will never come to pass.

These are lies.

The truth is . . .

There is nothing wrong with you.
There is no timeline that you *must* follow.

Every individual's timeline is unique and divinely inspired.

You are exactly where you need to be in this moment.

No schedule.
No deadlines.
No check boxes.

Just God writing the story of your life with you.

Can you trust, even when you can't see it or understand it, that the story is good?

I allow growth and change to occur in my life without resistance or fear.

Everything changes.
Everything passes.
Everything is reinvented.
You can choose to either flow with it or fear it.
What will you choose?

Even when I can't see it or understand it, I choose to trust that everything is working out exactly as it should.

Can you trust and rest in the knowledge that even if everything didn't go according to *your* plan, it went according to *the* plan for your life and that everything is working out exactly as it should?

I am fully loved even when people don't share or understand my dreams.

Not everyone will get you or your dreams.
And that's okay!

That's why ~~God gave~~ you have those dreams ~~to you~~ and ~~not to them~~. others do not.

It's not your job to play small and shrink back just to make others feel comfortable.

Your job is to make the most of this one precious life that you've been given and live it to your fullest potential.

Where are you holding back in your life because other people aren't supportive or don't understand you?

Let go.
You are loved.

I choose to see myself through the eyes of love.

So many of us try to punish ourselves into changing.
How's that going for you?

If being hard on yourself worked, it would have worked by now.

Let this be a new day. A new week. A fresh start.
An opportunity to do things differently from the way you've always done them.
Speak to and treat yourself like you would a small child or your best friend.
Choose to see yourself through the eyes of love.

I choose to find deep peace within myself.

Reminder: Stop searching outside yourself or looking to others for your peace.

Finding peace is an inside job.

It's a choice you make, just like choosing to get caught up in fear or worry.

The act of choosing gives your power back, rather than giving it away to a fleeting and oftentimes irrational emotion.

I release my need to constantly have the approval of others.

Your path and purpose are divinely inspired.
And you get to co-create a life with God that honors who you are and why you've been created, regardless of what other people think.

Instead of wasting time constantly trying to please and win the approval of others, spend more time connecting inward to hear what you're being called to do.

It is safe to be seen.

Isn't it amazing how many of us are hiding?
Hiding our true selves.
Hiding our gifts and talents.
Out of fear of being seen, heard and known.

Maybe there have been times in your life when you've shared yourself with someone and they weren't ready or able to receive you.

Please hear this . . .
That is *not* a reflection of your worth or value.
It's a reflection of where they were on their journey.
Don't allow one bad experience to cause you to retreat back into your shell.

The world doesn't need more people pretending, more people trying to fit into some cookie-cutter mold of who they think others want them to be.
We need you.
And all of your real, raw, beautiful mess.
We need you.

It is safe to be seen.

ALLY ROSE

I can face any situation that comes my way.

We've all had those moments where we've felt hurt, broken,
like a failure, even like our world was going to end or that we
couldn't possibly go on.
If you're reading this, it means you made it.
You survived.
You've done it before.
You'll do it again.

I accept the flow of abundance into my life.

Part of accepting abundance into your life is realizing that there is a flow and a dance to giving and receiving.

It's not about *always* being the giver.
And it's not about *always* being the receiver.

When we hoard or don't accept the help, people, places, things or opportunities that are sent our way to bless us, we block the flow of abundance in our lives.

This might seem weird, because who would reject abundance?

But there are many people who struggle with receiving without feeling guilty, feeling like they immediately have to repay the giver, or waste it or give it away because they don't feel worthy of receiving.

In reverse, there are many people who struggle with giving because they fear that they may never receive again.

Choose to step into the flow.
Say *yes* to abundance by participating in the dance and allowing your cup to be filled.
Only then can your cup overflow and fill others.
Trust that your cup will be filled and refilled again.

I am willing to let go of old beliefs, habits and patterns that no longer serve me.

Whatever God is up to in my life or yours, I know for sure it's something good.

Let go.
Unclench your fists.
Release anything that isn't for you, so that you can receive more than you could ever imagine.

I always have the freedom to choose.

We are the choices we make.
And every day that we wake up, we get to choose again.

To remain the same
Or do something different.

To stay
Or go.

To love
Or hate.

To speak up
Or stay silent.

To say yes
Or no.

I fully approve of who I am, even as I better myself.

Appreciate, love and nurture who you are now.
It's the foundation for who you are becoming.

I am divinely guided and inspired.

I don't know about you, but it takes a huge pressure off to know that there's a force far greater than myself that can see things from a much higher perspective than I can, guiding and inspiring my life.

Your job?
Tap into that divine inner knowing.
Listen, trust and follow through.

I accept things as they are and release everything in my life that is beyond my power to change.

Acceptance is not settling, failing or admitting defeat.
It is non-judgmental acknowledgment of what is.
No shame, blame or guilt.
It is a form of trust and surrender.
It is flow over force.
It is *the* starting point for healing, change and transformation.
What do you need to accept in your life?

Love, forgiveness and compassion are the foundation of my relationships.

We're human.
We fail, we fall, we make mistakes and then we get back up and hopefully do better next time.

Hate, judgment, shame and blame don't change hearts.
But love, forgiveness and compassion will.

This doesn't mean we allow toxic people into our inner circles ...
You can still have love and compassion for someone and have healthy and solid boundaries.

This is about recognizing that we're all just doing the best that we can, with what we know now and with where we are now on our path.

I commit to giving others what I want to receive.

We really never have any idea what's going on with a person behind the scenes.

If we treated everyone we met . . .

> the barista at our favorite coffee shop
> the stranger in line behind us at the grocery store with three screaming kids
> our co-workers
> our boss
> the janitor
> the cleaner
> our partner
> our friends
> our neighbors
> the homeless person begging for money as we walk down the street

. . . how we wanted to be treated ourselves, this world could be transformed by compassion and love.

I find safety and security inside of myself.

I've spent a lot of time in my life looking for safety and security outside of myself.

The problem with that is no one and nothing can truly give you anything before you give it to yourself.

Sure, external people and possessions can give you a false sense of security for a little while.

But no relationship, person, job or home can provide the true, grounded and anchored-in security we're all seeking.

So, how do we find it within ourselves?

To me, this means . . .

Connecting with and trusting in Divine Love, which is far greater and far more powerful than we are alone.

Not giving away our power to a person, place or thing.

And trusting ourselves to do what is for our highest good.

Don't allow the actions, reactions, opinions and judgments of others affect your decisions and how you feel about yourself or how you treat others.

What does finding inner safety and security mean to you?

My work has a profound impact on this world.

Your 'work' in life is not necessarily your *job* or something you get paid to do.
Some of us may be filled with gratitude because we love the work we get to do every day,
But even if you don't love your job, there's other important work that you are doing in your life.
People are watching you, even if they don't say anything.
You are impacting lives by how you live yours.
We are all connected and every choice we make has a ripple effect that goes far beyond our individual lives.
You are here for a reason.
Your life has purpose, meaning and value.

I draw from my inner strength and light.

I don't know what you are going through right now, but what I do know is that you have an inner strength and a light that burns within you. Maybe it's just a tiny ember right now, and all it needs is for you to tend to it, nurture it and fan it into flames.

I choose to participate fully in my day.

Have you ever felt like you're there, but not really there?
With people, but not really with them?
Eaten something, but not really tasted it?

I don't want to sleepwalk through my life and wake up one day
wondering how I got where I am.
I don't want to be constantly pulled by those nagging thoughts
from the past or the future and have to attend to them.
I want to be fully present in the day and in the moment that has
been given to me now.

Are you with me?

Choose to give yourself and the people you're with the gift of
fully participating in and experiencing your day.

I am worthy of love.

Inherent worthiness goes against everything our culture tells us. We have been taught that in order to be loved, we must be, do and have *all the things* to prove our worth.

This is a lie.
You are worthy.
And your worth is not based on anything you have done or will do.
You are worthy.
Simply because you exist.

I trust in the process of life and in the way it unfolds at this time.

When we plant seeds, we trust in the unseen process that has to happen underground in order for it to become something beautiful.

Similarly to the seed, the greatest moments of transformation in our lives often involve overwhelming change and coming wholly undone, in order for us to fully become who we've been created to be.

This process can be messy, ugly and scary.
It can look and feel like massive destruction.
The lesson is trusting the process in the middle of the mess.
It's so tempting to want to shortcut and bypass that messy part.
But if we dug up the seed before it came wholly undone and was ready to bloom, we'd never get to experience it in all of its goodness and glory.

Can you trust the process, every part of it? Knowing that when you do, you'll get to experience the fullness of who you are becoming.

I am open to the new and exciting changes and opportunities that are on their way to me.

the Universe

It is a *choice* to be open or closed to the work that ~~God~~ is trying to do in our lives.

~~S~~He's always moving, but ~~s~~He will never force us to do anything.

It's always your choice to say, "Yes, I am open to what you're doing in my life, to what you desire to change, to the opportunities that you have for me."

Or you can say *no* and stay right where you are.

To be honest, sometimes this is the more comfortable place to stay because we know it and because it feels so safe.

But know there's more for us, for you.

I don't know about you, but I don't want to miss out on what's coming my way . . .
Are you open too?

I release the struggle and choose peace instead.

Are you attached to the struggle?

Many of us are hooked on the idea that life has to be hard. We're addicted to complaining about the struggle and caught up in the fear involved.

What if we released the idea that it has to be hard? What if we could just let go of our attachments and let life be what it is?

Don't fight with life.
Flow with it.

I am good enough just as I am right now.

There's absolutely nothing wrong with wanting to learn, grow, transform and better yourself.
But in the process, make sure you take the time to appreciate love and nurture who you are now.
This current version of you is the foundation for who you are becoming.

I release the habit of criticizing myself.

Do you think you would grow, heal or change if the people in your life who are supposed to be supporting you were constantly criticizing you or beating you up for your decisions?

Obviously, the answer is no.
So I'm not sure why we believe that criticizing ourselves does us any good either.

The world is harsh enough as it is.
Why inflict more pain on yourself?

What would happen in your life if you replaced self-criticism with love, grace, gentleness and kindness?

Try it out.
You've got nothing to lose!

I focus on what I can control, and let go of what I can't.

Most people struggle to let go of control in relationships.
You're not alone!
I get it.
It's really hard.

But we are each only responsible for and able to control what we put out into the world and how we respond to what comes our way.

We can't control how someone will respond or react to us or what we share, no matter how carefully we craft the message or how good our intentions are.

As hard as it may be, we have to allow other people to have their own process.
To be on their own journey.
No matter where they are or whether we like it or not.

We can't change, heal or save people,
But we can support other people's healing journeys by doing our own healing work.

So focus on *your* journey, *your* actions, habits, patterns and behaviors.
Use all the time and attention that you've been spending on others and shift your focus back to yourself.
And let other people just *be* where they are.
You can send them love and well wishes.

But release the need to have control over their lives and how they show up in the world.

What relationship have you been struggling with lately? Who do you need to release right now?

I forgive myself, so I can regain inner peace.

When you won't forgive yourself, you hold yourself hostage to the past, and it makes it much harder to move forward.

Every version of who you were was necessary to get to where you are today.

So if and when you look back, can you look back with compassion and love instead of guilt, shame, anger or fear?

You can't change what happened, but you can always move forward in a new, better and different way.

I trust that Divine Love is working in me and through me.

There will always be days when you don't or can't trust yourself or your circumstances.

The true test is being able to believe, even on these difficult days, that Divine Love dwells within you and is working in your circumstances even when you can't see it, feel it or understand it.

If we can anchor in to the belief that we are being carried by a force of love that is so much greater than us, we will make it through.

I am fully loved, even when I'm in the messy middle.

The middle of any journey is often really messy and so we want to bypass it.

We may think, "If I could just be there on the other side, all would be okay."
But resisting and avoiding the middle is what keeps us stuck and playing small.

Because the middle is where the breakthroughs, growth and transformation happen.

It's important to love and embrace yourself throughout all parts of the journey, but especially in the middle.

If you're in the messy middle of anything right now, keep going.
And know that you are fully loved.
Right here, right now.
Just as you are.
Even when it doesn't look pretty and even when you feel like a mess.

I choose to believe that miracles still happen.

Many people think that miracles happen in these big amazing, life-altering, sirens-blaring and sparks-flying moments.

And that these moments don't happen all that often.

Could you choose to believe that miracles are happening all around us, all the time, in those small seemingly insignificant moments?

We're often so preoccupied with the past or future that our eyes aren't open to see the miracles unfolding right before us in the present moment.

What you look for you will find. *Magic*
I encourage you to open your eyes to the miracle moments happening all around you as you go through your days.

***I choose to see change as an
exciting opportunity for learning,
growth and discovery.***

We often view change as a loss of something, so we fight
against it.
Fighting against it doesn't work.
Flowing with change allows for new beginnings.
It allows us to lean deeper into the mystery of life.
It allows us to grow into more authentic versions of ourselves,
And discover parts of ourselves we've never known.

I release the habit of comparing myself to others.

Guess what?
That crazy socially constructed timeline that you think you need
to live your life by, the one that's making you feel like you're
somehow behind in life?
It's all made up!
There are no rules, my friend.

You get to create your own rules.
There is no roadmap.
Your path and your pace are perfect for you.
You are not late.
You are not early.
You are right on time.

I trust the process, honoring where I am right now.

We can spend so much time trying to get to the next good thing.
But often it's difficult to fully move forward until we've honored
where we are right now.
There are lessons to be learned in this stage of life and
in this season.
So allow yourself to feel the feelings.
Release any resistance to what's going on in your life right now.
And let life move through you.

I am worthy of new beginnings.

When something has not worked out as we expected it would,
When we feel like we have failed or that everything is
our fault . . .

Sometimes we will beat ourselves up and hold ourselves hostage
to the prison of old ways and unforgiveness of self.

We can convince ourselves that we are not worthy of
new beginnings.

It's time to let go of that belief.
It's time to be free.

Remaining a prisoner in our self-imposed cages will not change
what has gone before.

I am worthy of new beginnings.
You are worthy of new beginnings.
We are worthy of new beginnings.

I set healthy boundaries.

When we set healthy boundaries and stick to them . . .

We communicate love and care for ourselves, as well as others. We teach others how to treat us, and learn how to balance giving to ourselves, while also giving ourselves to others.

There is freedom within boundaries.

***There is a profound power in my stillness.
I cherish moments of silence.
I choose to make space for myself.***

We can hide in the noise.
We can hide in the hustle.
It's only when we stop, come out of hiding and make space that
we come face to face with ourselves and realize what we
truly need.
How will you make space for yourself today?

It is safe to slow down and allow myself to just be.

Your worth does not come from doing more.
We are human beings, not human doings.

Remember to take some time to just be.

Be with yourself.
Be with your thoughts.
Be with your family.
Be with your emotions.
Be with your friends.
Be in nature.
Be with God.

Just be.

I am safe within myself.

When you create a sense of safety and belonging within yourself,
You no longer need outside approval and validation
And you realize that you are home no matter where you go.

I am learning to own my power.
I deserve to feel free.

Have you ever given your power away?
In the past, I have.
More times than I can count.

I believed that someone outside of me—friends, lovers, coaches, healers, church community—knew better than I did what was best for me.

I made decisions from that place.
And I lost myself along the way.

At a certain point, I drew a line in the sand and said, "No more."
I went on a deeply transformative journey of remembering that deep down, I really do know what's best for me.
I learned how to trust myself again.

Taking back your power can be:
> Scary—because you can no longer blame others for your decisions. You have to own them and the outcomes—good or difficult. You must face things you would rather not face.
> Beautiful—because you love yourself and trust yourself more than ever.
> Liberating—because you will feel free from caring about what other people think about the decisions you make.

There's something so freeing about being able to make decisions from the depths of your soul without wavering even though you know others might question them.

ALLY ROSE

Because you know in your bones, without a shadow of a doubt, that it's the right choice for you.

You are powerful.
You are beautiful.
You deserve to feel free.

I am leaning in to hope and love.

So often we want to run, hide and shut down during difficult times or when we experience difficult emotions.

Can you accept the invitation from God to stay the course, to lean in to His hope and His love?

There is always that invitation to stay and face yourself, to own your emotions and lean in to God when you feel like you can't find or feel love and hope on your own.

And by trusting and leaning in, you can be transformed beyond your wildest imaginations.

Stay.
Lean in.
He's not finished yet.

I will carry on, and it will be beautiful.

The resiliency of the human spirit is one of the most amazing things we are ever privileged enough to witness.

Holding space for people while they share their stories, some heartbreaking, some devastating, has been my honor.

If we could sit down over a cup of coffee or tea, I would look you straight in the eyes and lovingly say . . .

"No matter what you're going through, no matter what has come your way during this season . . . You will carry on.
Because you are brave."

And you will be changed by it.
And it will be different.
And it might feel uncomfortable at first.
But eventually, it will be beautiful.

I will love myself, even on my bad days.

It may feel easier to love yourself when you're on top of the world, when you're killing it at *all the things*, when everything is flowing how it's 'supposed to' flow.

Yet what matters most is how you love yourself when you're feeling low, when you don't feel like getting out of bed, when you feel like things aren't flowing how they usually flow or how you feel like they 'should.'

This is life.
The ups and the downs, the ebb and the flow.

There will be days that we may not be able to show up for the world.
But if we can learn to show up for ourselves, we will never abandon or betray ourselves.

Here's how I show up for myself when I'm in a funk:

1. I ask myself, "What do I need most right now?"
    Note: I'm not asking, "How am I going to solve my whole life in this moment?"

2. I tune in to what I really need ...

Sometimes I need a nap.
Sometimes I need a shower.
Sometimes I need to connect with my mom or a dear friend.
Sometimes I just need to get started on something that I've been dragging my feet on ...

ALLY ROSE

The key is to focus on *one* thing.
Ask yourself *one* question, then listen.

Maybe a couple of answers will come up.
Just move forward with one of them.

Usually one small, loving step in the right direction is all you need
to remind yourself that you can do it and that this too shall pass.

How can you love yourself well on your bad days?

I will let love lead the way.

What would you do and who would you be if you weren't afraid?
How would your life look different if you let love in the
driver's seat?
How and where can you make one small change in your life this
week to let love take the lead, rather than allowing fear
control you?

***I love and accept myself
exactly the way I am.***

The world will only be transformed and lives will only be changed through radical love.
And I believe that this begins by learning how to love ourselves, radically, exactly as we are.
How will you love yourself well today?

I am coming home to myself.

The Invitation ...

For a period of time, during prayer and journaling time, I would
continually see a vision of God sitting in the big comfy chair in
my living room, next to the fire, inviting me to come home
to myself.

No, God was not a bearded man in a white robe.

It was more of an energy, an essence.

But the invitation to begin to take the journey was loud
and clear.

Of course, questions followed.

How do I do that? And what does it mean to come home
to myself?

I didn't have all the answers at the time.

All I knew was that I needed to say *yes* to this invitation.

What I've learned between then and now is that coming home
to myself meant creating a sense of safety, security, love, peace
and rest within myself.

No matter what's happening on the outside, I have cultivated
an inner sanctuary that I can always tap into and receive God's
love, peace and rest.

No matter where I go, I carry home with me.

The invitation is not just for me.

We are all called to come home to ourselves.

What does coming home to yourself mean to you?

And how can you begin to cultivate that in your life?

Thank you for reading.

Visit www.thedivinepause.com to connect further and/or receive inspiration and updates in your inbox.

Acknowledgments

I WANT TO thank Annick Ina, my beloved book doula and her team—I am 100% certain that we were Divinely led to one another. The moment I decided I was going to write this book, I knew I wanted to work with you. We hit it off immediately and without you, I know that this dream of mine would not be a reality. Sure, I could have pieced it together on my own, but you were the glue that held me together in this process. You went above and beyond in supporting me and for that I will be forever grateful.

About The Author

ALLY ROSE IS a mental health counselor who works with clients who are struggling with anxiety, depression, life transitions and relationship issues in her private practice in Kennett Square.

She is also the founder of Your Story Matters where she coaches women who are feeling stuck in their lives and/or businesses through her signature process of past, present, future coaching.

She guides her clients through a process of unlocking, clearing and rewriting past stories that are holding them back and no longer serving them.

Together they develop an individualized plan of action combining practical and spiritual tools that they can use in the present to help them move toward and create the lives they've always desired.